# Character is King
## God's Destination for You!

Workbook

Character is King Workbook
Published by Guy Thing Press
P.O. Box 827
Roanoke, TX 76262

This book or parts thereof may not be reproduced in any form, stored in a retrieval system, or transmitted in any form by any means - electronic, mechanical, photocopy, recording, or otherwise - without prior written permission of the publisher, except as provided by United States of America copyright law.

Guy Thing Press books my be purchased in bulk for educational, business, fund-raising, or sales promotional use. For more information, please contact Guy Thing Press.

Please visit us at www.guythingpress.com

Copyright © 2008 by Guy Thing Press
All Rights Reserved

*Printed in the United States of America*

ISBN-13:  978-0-9818337-5-0
ISBN-10:  0-9818337-5-6

Scripture taken from the New King James Version. Copyright © 1982 by Thomas Nelson, Inc. Used by permission. All rights reserved.

# Contents

Power of a Dream . . . . . . . . . . . . . . . . . . . . . . . . . . 1

It is All About Character . . . . . . . . . . . . . . . . . . . . . 9

God's Plan for Man . . . . . . . . . . . . . . . . . . . . . . . . 20

Dominion Commission . . . . . . . . . . . . . . . . . . . . . 25

God Works Through Patters . . . . . . . . . . . . . . . . . 33

Getting Wisdom . . . . . . . . . . . . . . . . . . . . . . . . . . 38

Without Hope, Faith is Unnecessary . . . . . . . . . . . 43

Kicking the Comfort Zone . . . . . . . . . . . . . . . . . . 46

Principles of Career Advancement . . . . . . . . . . . . 51

Picking up Bonuses Through Honoring God . . . . 58

Money: An Issue of the Heart . . . . . . . . . . . . . . . 65

# Chapter 1
Power of a Dream

**Character is King**

1. _____ are the secret power that overcomes every _____, _____, or _____ that stands between victory and us.

2. What is the difference between a dream and a fantasy?
   _____
   _____
   _____
   _____

3. Why was Gideon focused only on surviving when the angel came to him?
   _____
   _____

4. Usually when God speaks to you about your dream, your destiny, you are in _____ _____.

5. What was Gideon's dream really about? Who was the focus of it?
   _____
   _____

6. What must our dreams be based upon for them to endure?
   _____
   _____

7. Jesus told us that our care of others is the measure of our _____.

# Chapter 1
## Power of a Dream

8. God does everything according to a _____ based on a _____ of His kingdom.

9. We were created _____, not equally _____.

10. What determines our destiny?
    _____
    _____

11. What parts of ourselves make for excellence?
    _____
    _____

12. Why should we focus on improving our special endowments rather than our weaknesses?
    _____
    _____

13. What is the foundation of character?
    _____

14. God will give us all the time we need to develop our _____, and just because it may take a long time before we see an _____ on our investment does not mean that the _____ is not coming.

15. What does the word "valor" mean?
    _____

16. What two steps are involved in establishing discipline in one's life?
    _____
    _____
    _____
    _____

17. Why do we often hide our dreams and talents?
    _____
    _____

18. Both faith and fear attract. Faith attracts the _____; Fear attracts the
    _____.

19. Every dream is tested through the presence or lack of _____.

20. Why is it important to develop good character?
    _____
    _____
    _____

# Chapter 1
# Power of a Dream

# Key Point Review

1. How do we grow?
   _____
   _____

2. A genuine, authentic _____ will overcome and vanquish every _____.

3. We are not created _____ to others; We are created _____.

4. Every dream will be tested for its _____ and _____.

5. Discipline, or _____, is the essence of the kingdom.

6. _____ will always overcome resistance.

7. God made us to be _____.

Character is King

# Chapter 2
## It is all About Character

# Character is King

1. We are created in God's _____ and in His _____; therefore, we have the potential to share God's _____ attributes.

2. Maturation of character is a _____, not an event.

3. Where does knowing God come from?
   _____
   _____

4. What are the six things we can learn about how God manages His kingdom?
   _____
   _____
   _____
   _____
   _____
   _____

5. Why should we believe that God has something significantly better for us?
   _____
   _____

6. What is dominion?
   _____
   _____

7. What is one of the reasons the earth has not been covered with the glory of God?
   _____
   _____

# Chapter 2
## It is all About Character

8. What are the four techniques Satan uses in warring for our mind?

   _____
   _____
   _____
   _____
   _____

9. What defense should we incorporate to defend against Satan's tactics? What does this defense entail?

   _____
   _____
   _____
   _____

10. What will happen as we begin to meditate and obey God's word?

    _____
    _____

11. The man who meditates is "_____".

12. What two things are accomplished by confessing God's word?

    _____
    _____
    _____

13. We _____ our world by the words we speak.

14. Agreement is the place of _____. Disagreement is the place of _____.

15. What are the three ways that faithfulness is demonstrated?
_____
_____
_____
_____
_____
_____

# Chapter 2
## It is all About Character

# Key Point Review

1. We are created in the image of God, possessing His _____, _____, and _____.

2. God will never throw us into a fight that we _____.

3. _____ is necessary to please God.

4. God is constantly thinking of us and about how He can _____ _____.

5. Deception is doing what we believe to be the will of God in "_____."

6. How is faithfulness measured?
   _____
   _____

7. _____ is your destiny.

# Chapter 3
## God's Plan for Man

**Character is King**

1. What is required for doing things God's way?
   _____
   _____

2. Why is work important to God?
   _____
   _____
   _____

3. We are only _____ of those things with which He has entrusted us.

4. What does it mean to fellowship with God?
   _____
   _____

5. How are all of us created special?
   _____
   _____

6. What is one of Satan's major deceptions?
   _____
   _____

7. God did not make us to be _____. He made us for _____.

# Chapter 3
## God's Plan for Man

Answer the following self-inventory questions.

8. What do I do well?

   _____
   _____
   _____

9. What do I enjoy doing?

   _____
   _____
   _____

10. What do other people say I do well?

    _____
    _____
    _____

11. What opportunities do I have now?

    _____
    _____
    _____

12. In what areas have I experienced rapid learning?

    _____
    _____
    _____

13. In what areas have I experienced glimpses of excellence?
   _____
   _____
   _____

14. The rewards that we experience are based on our _____, not on how many talents we possess.

15. We are only held accountable for what God has _____.

16. There will always be people who try to keep us at the level of _____.

17. What must we prove before God will give us the Kingdom?
   _____
   _____

18. How is the enemy trying to curse us when he attacks us with low self-esteem?
   _____
   _____

# Chapter 3
## God's Plan for Man

# Key Point Review

1. Our _____ is tied to our gifting.

2. God is a _____; He is not in a hurry.

3. Fellowship with God is when we _____ and _____ steward the gifts he has entrusted to us.

4. Reaching our fullest potential in life is found when we focus and improve our _____.

5. Increase only comes when we are _____ and _____ in waiting.

6. To go to the next area of life, we must be willing to _____ _____.

7. Once we have done the will of God, we must wait for the _____.

# Chapter 4
Dominion Commission

# Character is King

1. Knowing God entails total _____ and some _____.

2. What was being said in the commission found in Genesis 1:26-28?
   _____
   _____
   _____

3. What two branches did the Israeli government have and what was their purpose?
   _____
   _____
   _____
   _____

4. What happened before kings and priests served God in the capacities He wanted them to serve?
   _____
   _____

5. Why does it make sense to believe that more people would be anointed as kings instead of priests?
   _____
   _____
   _____
   _____
   _____

# Chapter 4
## Dominion Commission

6. Why did the Romans feel threatened by the "ekklesia" that Christ had put together?
   _____
   _____
   _____

7. Why must there be cooperation between kings and priests?
   _____
   _____
   _____

8. According to the book, what offices are the equivalent of the following biblical elders found in the church?

   Apostle = _____
   Prophet = _____
   Evangelist = _____
   Pastor = _____
   Teacher = _____

9. Power and destiny come through _____.

10. How do problems reveal our character?
    _____
    _____
    _____
    _____

11. What are the three differences between wealth and riches?
   _____
   _____
   _____

12. Why has God given us the power to gain riches and wealth?
   _____
   _____
   _____

13. What are the four aspects of our responsibility as stewards?
   _____
   _____
   _____
   _____

14. God's pattern is _____, _____, _____.

15. Most of the problems we face are _____ to be learned, and most of our trials are to prepare us for _____.

Chapter 4
Dominion Commission

# Key Point Review

1. God created us for His _____, and He wants us to cover the earth with His _____.

2. The church and the kingdom are not _____ terms.

3. All work is _____.

4. _____ does not make the man; it merely reveals the man for what he really is.

5. _____ are something we have; _____ is someone we are.

6. Wealth is created by obedience to God's _____, _____, and _____.

7. _____ character is your destiny.

**Character is King**

Character is King

# Chapter 5
God Works Through Patterns

# Character is King

1. What job and responsibility do the kings have to the church?
   _____
   _____
   _____

2. What are the spheres of government that are not affected by the church and why?
   _____
   _____
   _____
   _____

3. What is the role of the priest?
   _____
   _____
   _____

4. What is the role of the kings?
   _____
   _____
   _____

5. How were the roles of king and priest clearly defined in Israel?
   _____
   _____
   _____
   _____

# Chapter 5
## God Works Through Patterns

6. Kings and priests never attempted to remove the other from his office lest they _____ _____.

7. We are _____ in the priesthood and _____ in the kinghood.

8. How do you think business people feel when they are classified as "second-rate believers"?
_____
_____
_____
_____

9. Without the blessings of God, there is no _____.

10. What happens when we do not have a strong mission from God?
_____
_____
_____

11. Priests generate _____ faster than they can generate _____.

12. What is the first step in developing our kingship?
_____
_____

13. What is the second step in developing our kingship?
_____
_____

14. What five steps were involved in the king copying the law?
_____
_____
_____
_____
_____
_____

15. What is the third step in developing our kingship?
_____
_____

# Chapter 5
## God Works Through Patterns

# Key Point Review

1. _____ handle the glory of God and _____ establish economic dominion.

2. Your _____ can take you where your _____ cannot sustain you.

3. What does the anointing of the Holy Spirit symbolize?
_____
_____

4. Kings should read _____ in the morning for wisdom and _____ at night for courage.

5. _____ is your destiny.

# Chapter 6
Getting Wisdom

**Character is King**

1. According to Proverbs 4:7, what is the most important thing we can do?
   _____
   _____

2. What is wisdom?
   _____
   _____
   _____

3. What two types of scripture do the Bible speak about?
   _____

4. The reason for lack of wisdom is that there is no _____.

5. What traps us in our own human wisdom?
   _____
   _____

6. _____ indicates independence from God; _____ indicates dependence on God.

7. When should we ask God for wisdom? What precedes our need for wisdom?
   _____
   _____

# Chapter 6
## Getting Wisdom

8. Why does God actively oppose pride?

9. How is our love of God evidenced in our humility?

10. What is humility?

Chapter 6
Getting Wisdom

# Key Point Review

1. Pursuing _____ is the most important thing we can do in life.

2. The _____ is the wisdom of God.

3. _____ precedes God's grace in our life.

4. _____, _____, _____, _____ is the pattern for dominion in the earth.

5. What is wisdom?
   _____
   _____

# Chapter 7
Without Hope, Faith is Unnecessary

**Character is King**

1. What is hope?
   _____
   _____

2. What is faith?
   _____
   _____

3. What is described by the word hope?
   _____
   _____
   _____

4. In what circumstance would one be unable to please God?
   _____
   _____

# Chapter 7
## Without Hope, Faith is Unnecessary

# Key Point Review

1. _____ is the fuel that keeps the dream alive?

2. Hope that pleases God is birthed from the _____ of God.

3. Every great _____ is done by hope.

4. We worship the God of _____.

5. Without hope _____ is unnecessary.

**Character is King**

Character is King

# Chapter 8
Kicking the Comfort Zone

# Character is King

1. Just because we have put in the time does not mean that we have _____.

2. How do we grow?
   _____
   _____
   _____

3. In what two ways can we get out of the comfort zone?
   _____

4. The primary mentoring responsibility of any parent is to our own _____.

5. As we _____ and _____ in the word, it will dramatically change every area of our lives.

6. How does prayer produce intimacy?
   _____
   _____
   _____

7. How should we view our strengths and what should we do with them?
   _____
   _____
   _____

# Chapter 8
## Kicking the Comfort Zone

8. What is the first myth regarding strengths and weaknesses as explained in the book?
_____
_____
_____

9. What is the second myth?
_____
_____

10. The _____ of the Holy Spirit gives us the edge, or the _____.

11. What four ways does the anointing of the Holy Spirit help us in the workplace?
_____
_____

**Character is King**

# Chapter 8
## Kicking the Comfort Zone

# Key Point Review

1. Why is living in the comfort zone easy?
   _____

2. All growth occurs _____ of the comfort zone.

3. How do we get out of our comfort zone?
   _____

4. _____ wants us to focus on our strengths. _____ wants us to focus on our weaknesses.

5. What happens when we try to improve our weaknesses?
   _____

6. What happens when we improve upon our strengths?
   _____

# Chapter 9
Principles of Career Advancement

# Character is King

1. How is God's plan revealed to us?
   _____
   _____

2. Acting upon God's principles starts with _____ and _____.

3. Why should we focus on building our character and not our personality?
   _____
   _____
   _____

4. What happens when we walk in the Word of God?
   _____
   _____
   _____
   _____

5. What four things has God given us for our lives?
   _____
   _____
   _____

6. What initiates fellowship?
   _____
   _____
   _____

# Chapter 9
## Principles of Career Advancement

7. Why should we feed our spirits every day?

8. What is the threefold definition of faith?

9. What must we believe about God to please Him?

10. What are some of the scriptures that point out what is expected under diligence?

11. What are some of the scriptures that deal with meditation?

12. _____ is a by-product of a relationship with God.

13. Why does God want us to prosper?
_____
_____

14. What is the central issue of our lives?
_____
_____

15. What advantages does the anointing of God give us in our lives?
_____
_____
_____

16. In what ways does God help us in everyday decisions?
_____
_____
_____
_____

17. Why are most of us not experiencing God's best?
_____
_____

# Chapter 9
## Principles of Career Advancement

18. What does it mean to "forget a failure"? How can we know when we have forgotten a failure?
　
　
　
　

19. What is a reason we have difficulty forgetting?
　
　

20. What does forgiveness mean?
　
　

21. In what four areas must we prove ourselves to be counted as faithful by God?
　
　
　
　

22. _____ will prevent us from reaching our God-ordained destiny.

**Character is King**

**Character is King**

# Chapter 9
## Principles of Career Advancement

# Key Point Review

1. God created us for _____, and for the work of our hands to be _____.

2. All true happiness and success are born out of a _____.

3. God has given us _____ to live by, _____ to believe in, _____ to follow, and _____ to obey.

4. _____ in every area of life brings reward.

5. We must forget the _____ and _____ of the past before we can embrace the future.

6. _____ is the foundation of our character.

7. Our _____ represents our life.

Character is King

# Chapter 10
## Picking Up Bonuses Through Honoring God

**Character is King**

1. God is neither partial nor _____, doubleminded nor _____.

2. Doing the will of God is likened unto _____
   _____.

3. What happens if we do God's will with patience?
   _____

4. On what does the Kingdom of God operate?
   _____
   _____
   _____

5. In what four areas can we honor God more?
   _____
   _____

6. How can looking at our checkbooks reveal where our heart is?
   _____

7. What is your obedience proof of?
   _____
   _____

8. What can hinder the prayers of a man?
   _____

# Chapter 10
## Picking Up Bonuses Through Honoring God

9. What does a wife's relationship with her husband satisfy?

10. What must a man do to meet this need?

11. What mistake do some men make after marriage that causes their wife to become less submissive?

12. Honoring your parents financially is a _____.

**Character is King**

**Character is King**

**Chapter 10
Picking Up Bonuses Through Honoring God**

# Key Point Review

1. After we have done the will of God, we must have _____ before we will receive the promise.

2. God will honor only those who _____.

3. We honor God when we give _____ to His work.

4. Men must honor their wives as _____ or their prayers will not be answered.

5. Honoring our parents means to help them _____.

**Character is King**

# Chapter 11
Money: An Issue of the Heart

# Character is King

1. What is involved in economics?
   _____
   _____

2. _____ is probably the most important material resource in the Kingdom of God.

3. Proper stewardship of material resources, i.e., money, establishes _____ and _____.

4. If no one is influenced, there is no _____.

5. What we believe about money will _____ or _____ it.

6. So long as we view God as our _____, he will give us as much money as we can handle.

7. God's top priority is the _____.

8. What five spheres of government do we have in the Kingdom of God?
   _____
   _____
   _____

9. What were the ekklesia?
   _____
   _____
   _____

# Chapter 11
## Money: An Issue of the Heart

10. What two things must we understand for the church of today to operate as the ekklesia did?

11. What is the purpose of prosperity?

12. What does the term "reciprocation" mean? How does it apply to the kingdom?

13. What does the term "substance" mean? How does it apply to us?

14. Before God will promote you or give you increase in your life, what will He do to you?

15. What influences the size of the harvest you will reap?

16. _____ precedes increase.


17. What must you get in order for God to bless you and take you to the next level? How can you work in your life to bring about this blessing?
   _____
   _____
   _____
   _____


18. How do you control your destiny when you are sowing into the kingdom?
   _____
   _____

# Chapter 11
## Money: An Issue of the Heart

# Key Point Review

1. Money is important to God because it shows the condition of our _____ and tests our _____.

2. The pattern of _____ and _____ governs life.

3. God requires of us faithful _____.

4. He tests our stewardship with the _____, to see if He can trust us with more.

5. It is God's will that we live in _____.

# Resources of Interest

**Character is King**
*Dr. John Binkley*

*It's a Guy Thing: Character is King* takes you on your dream journey. There is a place called destiny that we all jouney to. We all have ideas, dreams and vision for what life should be. This book lays out a plan for that journey to realizing your dreams, to your destiny.

**Let's Talk About Sex**
*Dr. John A. King*

Let's face it. Sexuality is all around us. It's even on billboards, and television commercials. Sadly, It's a topic many men have to discover on their own because too many churches or pastors won't touch it. *Let's Talk About Sex* was written so men no longer have to discover the answers to the tough questions about sex on their own.

**Now to Next**
*Dr. John A. King*

What does the next generation church look like? Who are the people that will be involved in the next generation church? How will it come about?

Those are some of the questions answered in Dr. King's newest release, *Now to Next: Blueprint for a Christian Revolution.*

**Helping Guys Become Men, Husbands, and Fathers**
*Dr. John A. King*

*It's a Guy Thing* takes you on the journey of fatherhood. Dr. King shows you, in this book, the skills neccesary to become a good father. He shows you what can happen when a father is absent or simply not active in a child's life.
Being a male is a matter of birth. Being a man is a matter of choice. This book will help you make that choice.

To see all the titles available through Guy Thing Press, visit us online at www.guythingpress.com

# Resources of Interest

**Business By The Book**
*Dr. John A. King*

The world's greatest handbook on leadership, economic and social excellence is not found in schoolbooks, but is Scripture. The principles in this book are tried, proven and resilient over centuries. Christ bet His life on it, and so can you.

**Show Me the Money**
*Dr. John A. King*

Time Magazine asked, "Does God want you to be rich?" The answer to that question is simply "No, God wants you to be *wealthy*." In *Show Me the Money*, you will learn the fundamentals of creating and using wealth in God's kingdom.

**Achieving Authentic Wealth**
*Jeff McLoud*

We need a vision that goes beyond our ability to be consumers only. A vision so big, so powerful, that we cannot even accomplish it in our own lifetime - a vision founded from the very heartbeat of God. We could see the vision fulfilled if we ask ourselves a simple question: "How can we achieve twice as much with half the money?"

**Creating a Better Life**
*Erik A. Kudlis*

In this easy to read manual, educator and administrator turned national and international businessman, Erik Kudlis, identifies three vital keys you must know and use, given by God Himself, that unlock the doors to the life God always wanted you to have.

To see all the titles available through Guy Thing Press, visit us online at www.guythingpress.com

# Further Resources

### The Godly Man Curriculum

The Godly Man Curriculum is the latest development of the International Men's Network. This training curriculum is designed to train men from all walks of life and give them a firm foundation of doctrine and Godly knowledge. This curriculum is available both over the internet for individual study or by DVD for seminars, Sunday schools, and men's meetings. With up to 7 hours of video teaching divided over numerous topics, the Godly Man Curriculum is an excellent tool that you can build your classes upon and grow yourself and your people.

### Building Iron Men & Life As Leaders Networks

The Building Iron Men and Life as Leaders networks are two of IMN's finest resources. Each network provides you with a new teaching every month that will challenge and encourage you to grow. The Building Iron Men network features three teachings in both CD and DVD format that focus on your men, while the Life as Leaders network provides you with three CDs that teach you leadership principles you can use in every area of your life.

Both networks are phenomenal tools that are vital assets to any church and discipleship program.

For more information about these and other resources, visit us online at www.imnonline.org

## Also check out these websites for great resources and training materials.

International Men's Network
www.imnonline.org

Guy Thing Press
www.guythingpress.com

The International Men's Network was founded by Dr. John A. King. Our purpose as an organization is to help men not only grow to become the leaders their families and churches need, but also become men of God that make a lasting impact on those around them.

IMN is a missionary organization to the men of the world. We are committed to:

- Inspire all men to rise to a high standard of biblical manhood.
- Encourage them to excel in their roles as men, leaders, husbands, and fathers.
- Challenge them to be contributors to society and set an example based upon a biblical value system that will benefit this generation and lay a solid foundation for the next.

As an organization, the International Men's Network is dedicated to providing and hosting the best resources for men, whether it comes from teachings and lessons on CD/DVD format or via a conference that will teach men principles that will help them become more influential and effective in their lives.

For more information about IMN and its mission, visit us online at www.imnonline.org or contact us via phone at 817.993.0047

The Christian Life Center was founded by Dr. John King and his wife, Beccy. With a vision to preach the gospel of Jesus Christ with unashamed passion and uncompromising truth, Christian Life Center aims to raise up the next generation of leaders to move into all the world and proclaim the truth of Christ to the lost and broken.

Located in the Keller, TX area, the Church sits in the prime location to reach the community and the people therein. The Church desires to give back to the community by providing outreaches to better and enrich its inhabitants. From kickboxing classes that are aimed at teaching children and adults self-defense to special service that commemorate and honor our country's war-time heroes, the church strives to bring a living Jesus to a dying world by new and imaginative means that will bless and change lives.

For more information about Christian Life Center and the resources it offers, visit the website at www.clctx.org

www.ingramcontent.com/pod-product-compliance
Lightning Source LLC
LaVergne TN
LVHW081544060526
838200LV00048B/2205